three different ways to wear a scarf

a vintage postcard

a tantalizing pâtisserie window

a bird's-eye view

a working barge on the Seine

a baker at work

an apricot galette

an arched doorway

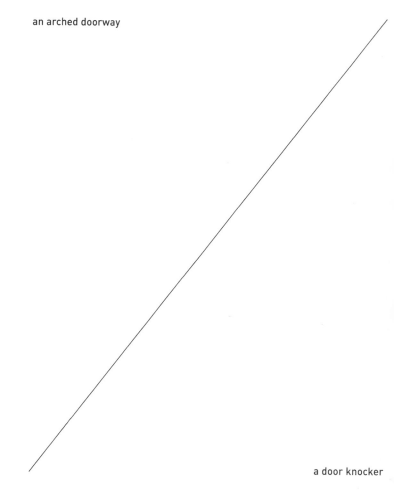

a door knocker

Chanel N°5

a Baccarat crystal vase

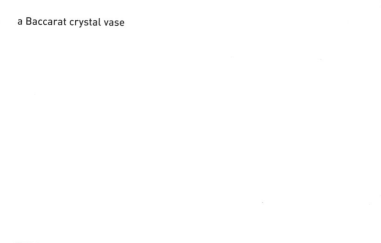

a "Pick Up After Your Dog" sign

a DJ in the zone | a sommelier

a two-euro coin	a basket of chanterelles
a lingerie ad	a madeleine

a bobo on a bicycle

---

endives

---

autumn leaves

Orangina

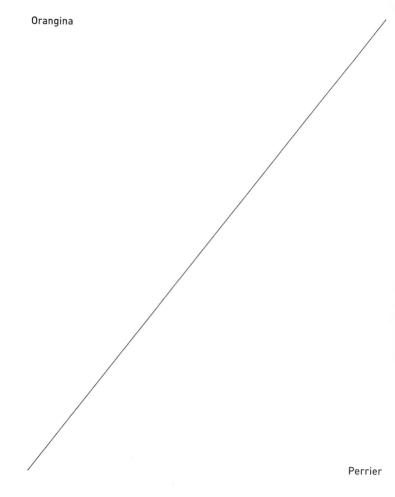

Perrier

tulip season

---

a "Do Not Disturb" sign

a carafe of house wine

a bunch of salami hanging
from the ceiling

a box of chocolates from Fauchon

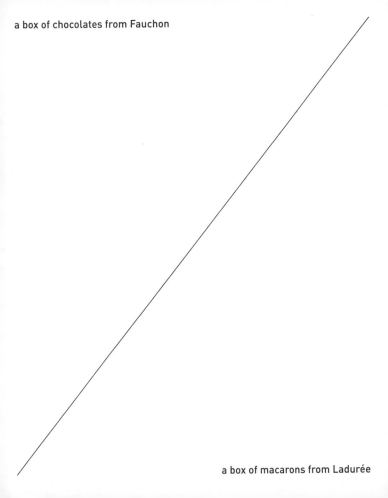

a box of macarons from Ladurée

the Louvre Pyramid

the interior of Montmartre's Au Lapin Agile

a cognac

absinthe

a bowl of olives

a bunch of leeks

an enfilade

___

box seats at the Palais Garnier opera house

___

a striped sailor's sweater

a rooftop garden

Hemingway and Fitzgerald knocking back a few

_____

a brass band on the street

a snow-dusted statue

---

a *brocante*

---

the Left Bank

a platter of alcoholic *pâtes de fruits*

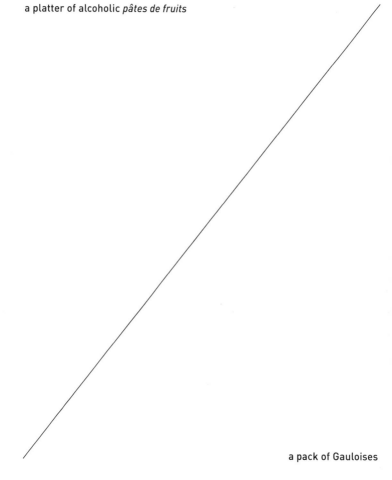

a pack of Gauloises

a candy kiosk

a bustling street market

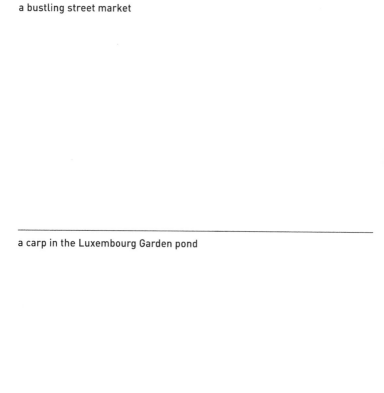

a carp in the Luxembourg Garden pond

a French press pot of coffee

a boy in a beret

an ashtray

moules-frites

a postmodern dessert

an ancient elevator

joggers in the Luxembourg Garden

---

a Cartier watch

a flea market hustler

a "monuments of Paris" charm bracelet

having a drink at the Hemingway Bar at the Ritz

a cheese plate

a stolen kiss

a modern floral arrangement

a Roman amphitheater

a French bulldog

---

a chiffon gown

an éclair

a steaming choucroute

an awning

a Diptyque candle

a French 75 cocktail

a quiche Lorraine

a bellboy

a portrait painter

a scooter

Christmas lights

a shop window on the Avenue Montaigne

a corset

a devilish smile

a *chocolat chaud* on a cold winter's day

---

a schoolchild in uniform

---

a medieval wood-framed house

a display of fancy lotions

a basket of tiny wild strawberries

a Barbour jacket

a cobbler

a dish of rough-cut brown sugar cubes

a haberdashery

---

a marriage proposal

a hip record shop

a corner florist

a platter of canapés

radishes with salt and butter

a *sandwich au jambon*

a cooking class at Le Cordon Bleu

a distinguished granny with a shopping basket

---

a ramekin of crème brûlée

---

a fishmonger

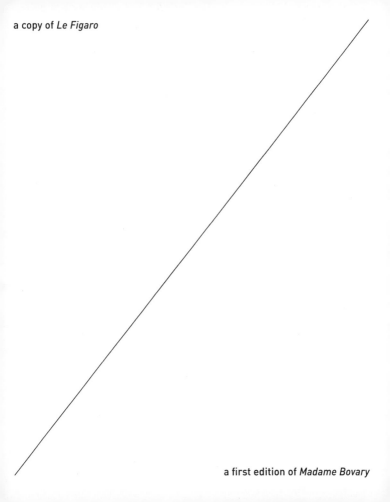

a copy of *Le Figaro*

a first edition of *Madame Bovary*

a brazenly illegally parked car

a day at the races

a courtesan | a street artist

a room in the Vampire Museum

a dog in a purse

a crate of melons	a Sorbonne student
a bottle of Evian	a Citroën Deux Chevaux

a tatty souvenir shop

a fashion show finale

a straight-backed bike rider

---

a fountain pen

---

chestnut trees along the Seine

a doorman

---

a topiary garden

---

a gendarme

a perfectly golden brioche

---

a flower-filled bicycle basket

---

a hand-scribbled restaurant check

a cancan dancer | a fleur-de-lis

a Kelly bag | a flute of Champagne

a chess game in the park

---

a food truck

---

a hatbox

a doll maker's studio

---

a Gallic rooster

an old-fashioned shop sign

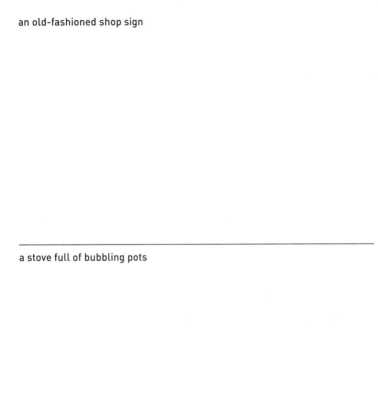

a stove full of bubbling pots

a gaggle of foreign students

---

a handful of old French francs

---

a concierge's doorway

a fashion faux pas

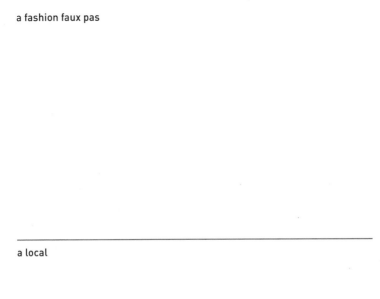

a local

a French stamp

———————————————————————————————————

the gilded Joan of Arc statue

a grande dame

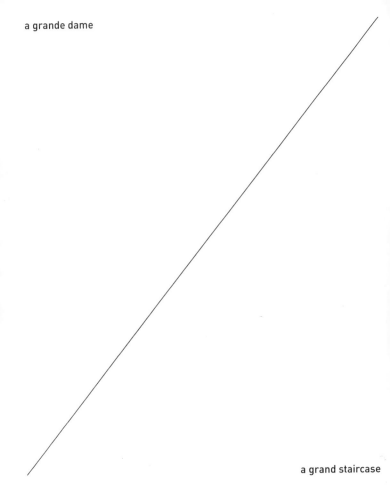

a grand staircase

a glass of rosé	a dress with a bustle
a flirt	a handsome produce vendor

a luggage cart of Vuitton suitcases

a *guinguette* on the Seine

a jar of cornichons

a lineup of Vélib' bicycles

---

a glimpse of a courtyard beyond a colorful door

---

a kitchen knife

a fashion student	a jet-set shopper
a jovial butcher	a mannequin

a chocolatier's Easter display

---

a jewelry designer's worktable

a feathered burlesque costume

a Petit Bateau onesie

a love letter

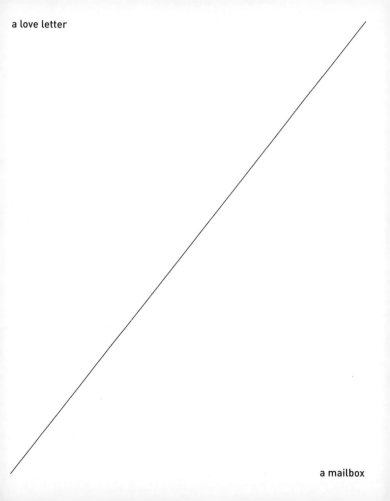

a mailbox

a harpist

a Pierrot doll

a jar holding sugar packets

a lace fan

a man wearing plaid pants	a Bon Marché shopping bag
a little black dress	a croissant

F. Scott and Zelda

a concept shop

a jazz bar in Montmartre

a kir royale cocktail at Les Deux Magots

---

first time at the flea market

---

a loaf of Poilâne bread

| a fountain | a magazine rack |

a honey shop

a lipstick kiss on a napkin

performing for tips on a Metro car

a painted ceiling

---

a bridge covered with locks

---

a man reading *Le Monde*

a mime

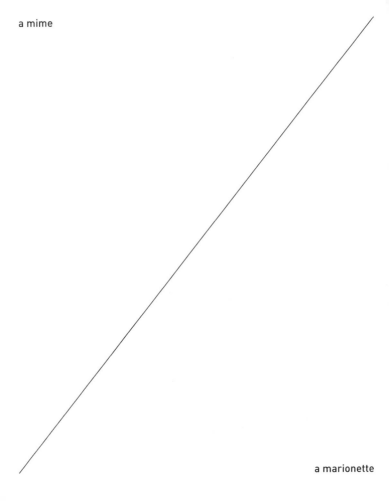

a marionette

the Lost Generation

a river barge garden

a map of the arrondissements

French baroque

a local designer's shop

a grand hotel lobby

a Mariage Frères tea canister

a plastic shopping caddy

---

a marked-up page of *Pariscope*

a leather jacket	roasting chickens
a street performer	a chef's toque

a Mercedes taxi

a cask of wine

a nervous, exquisitely coiffed little dog

a musical instrument repair shop

a church organ

---

a warmly lit bistro on the first cold night of fall

a Metro train at 2 a.m.

a palette and paintbrush

a falafel sandwich

a mille-feuille

hanging copper pots

a monochromatic street performer

---

a regular at the corner café

---

a pedal cab

a potted palm	a sea urchin
a pastis	a palmier

a literary lunch at Le Procope

a Metro map

a trash-chic bar scene

---

a change tray

---

a North African street market

a paddle boat in Versailles's Grand Canal

---

studded ankle booties

Camembert

an aristocrat

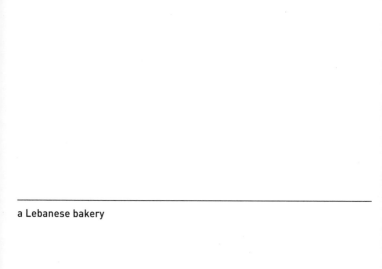

a Lebanese bakery

a nightclub dance floor

a perfectly behaved dog seated in a restaurant

a nun | a Gothic church

a picnic on the Pont des Arts

a carousel

a Carte Orange

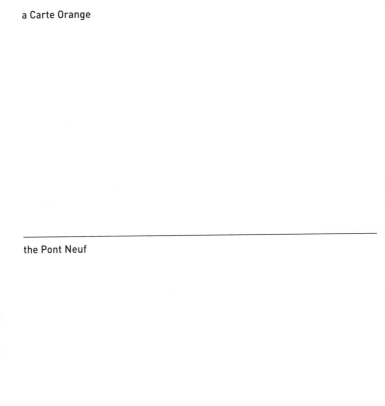

the Pont Neuf

a secret garden

a pixie haircut

a wine label

a pharmacy sign

a donkey ride in the park

a medieval fortress

a rococo ceiling

an art gallery opening

a "No Parking" sign

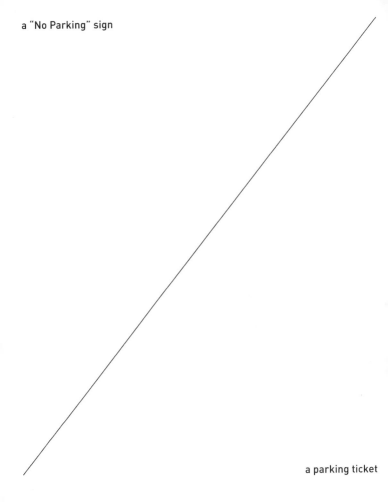

a parking ticket

a pot of anti-aging lotion	a double-decker bus
a rhinestone brooch	a philosophy professor

a concert in the park

---

a postmodern light fixture

---

a rude salesperson

a lovers' tryst

a child in a peacoat

mansard roofs

a poodle

shoes in a shoe store

---

a romantic garret

---

a protest march

a concert flyer

a stained-glass rose window

| a postcard rack | a narrow cobblestoned street |

a salted caramel ice cream cone
from Berthillon

a flirty summer dress

a romantic candlelit dinner

a cabaret act

a raspberry tart

a ramekin of sea salt

a diamond bauble

a coaster

a powder puff

a Renault

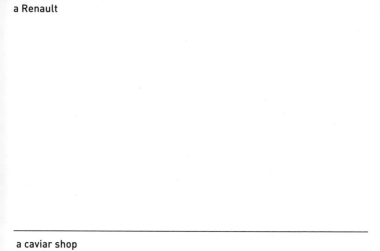

a caviar shop

a sea of umbrellas

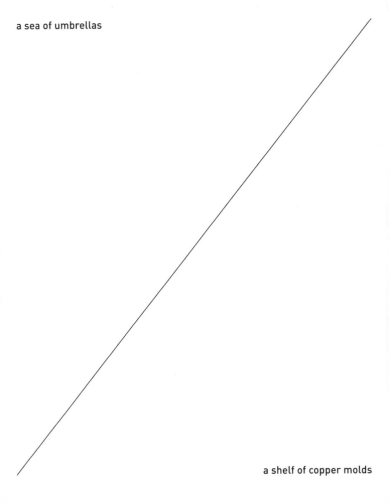

a shelf of copper molds

a staircase in Montmartre

a corner grocer

a snob

a rose arbor on the Promenade Plantée

---

a poet

a couple on a scooter

a salade niçoise

a sidewalk chalk artist | a bow-tied waiter

a beautifully dressed child | a dapper gentleman in a beret

Dior's New Look

a security guard	a pile of euros
a lemon tart	a straw market tote bag

a rugby game on the Invalides Lawn

---

a string of pearls

---

the gardens of Bagatelle

a pickpocket

a silver coffee pot

a Smart car

a roasted-chestnuts vendor

a houseboat

---

a plush hotel bathrobe

the ghost of the Bastille

---

a fireman's ball

a soufflé

---

a phone number scrawled on a napkin

---

the Obelisk of the Place de la Concorde

a sleek chignon

a *papeterie*

a cat in a window

a tiered platter of oysters at La Coupole

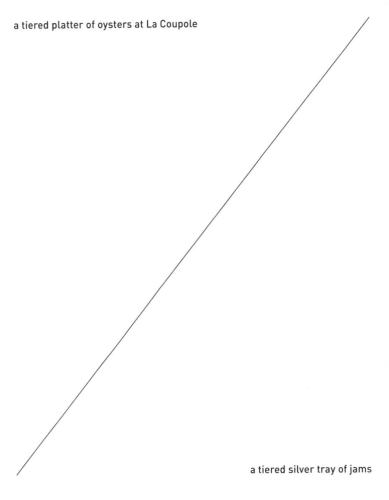

a tiered silver tray of jams

a stack of baguettes | a stack of *canelés*

the Grande Arche de la Défense

taking to the sewers

a tartine

a rattan café chair

a thinning cream
advertisement

a used Metro ticket

a chunky gold bracelet

---

a stuffed gazelle from Deyrolle

Saint-Sulpice's mismatched towers

an antique corkscrew

---

a vintage French silk scarf

---

a very old bicycle

a turret

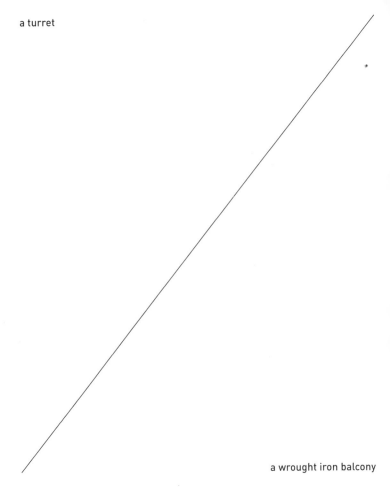

a wrought iron balcony

a stylish couple out for a stroll

---

an old cannon

a cook in an apron

a tube of red lipstick

a vintage steamer trunk

a peekaboo view of the
Eiffel Tower

a flea market treasure

a wedge of triple-crème Délice de Bourgogne

a nanny pushing an old-fashioned pram

a tapestry

a crêpe vendor

a three-star chef

---

a three-star restaurant

a puppet theater

Amélie

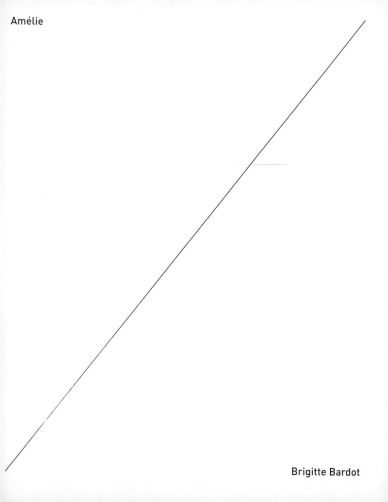

Brigitte Bardot

Louis XIV's wig

_____

a trompe l'oeil ceiling

a vegetable stall

---

a wannabe model

---

a flower box

a vertical garden

a Wallace fountain

a woman in a Chanel suit,
walking her dog

an American in Paris

a traffic jam

---

a window framed by heavy silk curtains

a surly waiter

a violinist

a tourist in running shoes

a writer in a café

Paris in the rain

a fur coat

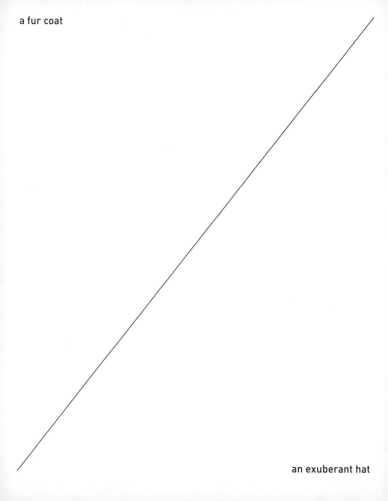

an exuberant hat

a chic hair salon

a wine cellar

_____

an alligator-skin bag

the Musée d'Orsay clock

a stylish clutch

a zinc counter

runners on the embankment

a *bateau mouche*

artful graffiti

a couture wedding gown

a bottle of nail polish

lost at Châtelet Metro station

an elegant table setting

an antique chair

an ornate gilded mirror

Bastille Day fireworks

beach volleyball by the Seine

boating in the Bois de Boulogne

an over-the-top floral display

an art nouveau Metro station

an amuse-bouche

a monogrammed handkerchief

an enamel street sign bolted to a building

bric-a-brac

a New Year's Eve soirée

---

an artist's studio in Belleville

a pepper grinder | a lamppost

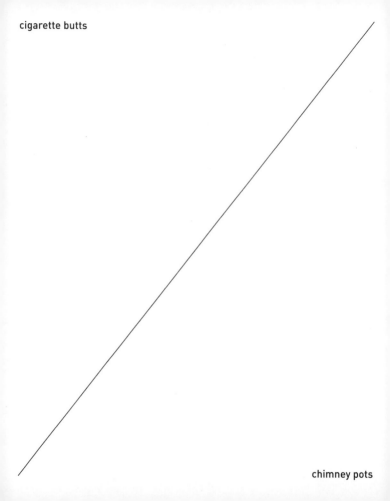

cigarette butts

chimney pots

an art nouveau newspaper kiosk

an elaborately folded napkin

an old-fashioned toy shop

an iced seafood platter

a synagogue

an opinionated hair stylist

---

an existentialist

an international banker

cabaret dancers in their dressing room

sexy lingerie

romance

---

a Toulouse-Lautrec bohemian party

Angelina's famous hot chocolate

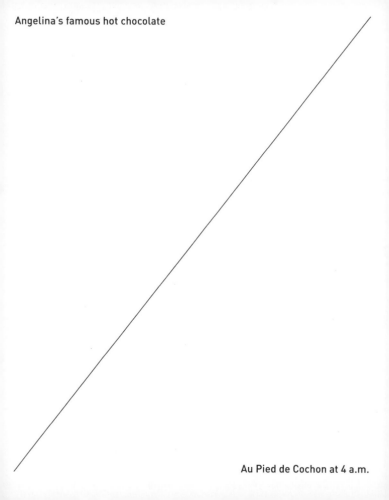

Au Pied de Cochon at 4 a.m.

cool cats at Café Charbon

Frédéric Chopin and George Sand in love

an overpriced aperitif with a view

---

a candelabra

a wrapped caramel | an intellectual

an organ grinder | a café au lait

a huge chandelier

cubism

a diplomat having pizza

celebrating the release of the Beaujolais Nouveau

an upscale butcher shop

---

an oversized boho tote bag

an urn overflowing with flowers

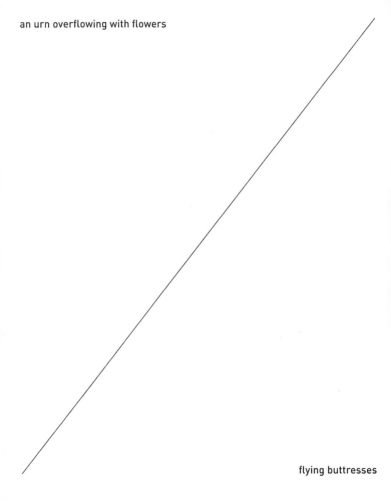

flying buttresses

an old-school wine bar

_____

cuff links

_____

daredevil on a scooter

Balzac's house

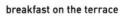

breakfast on the terrace

cinema *en plein air*

Chagall's ceiling at the Palais Garnier opera house

Paris in the snow

Degas's ballerinas

Louboutins

dancing beneath the Pont Alexandre III

storming the Bastille

Fashion Week frenzy

enjoying a smoke

dancing till dawn

in love

an artisan's studio on the Viaduc des Arts

drinking alone

an "I [heart] Paris" apron

a vintage perfume bottle

gilded cherubs

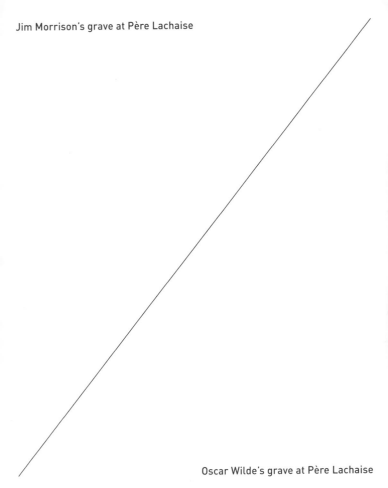

Jim Morrison's grave at Père Lachaise

Oscar Wilde's grave at Père Lachaise

lilies of the valley

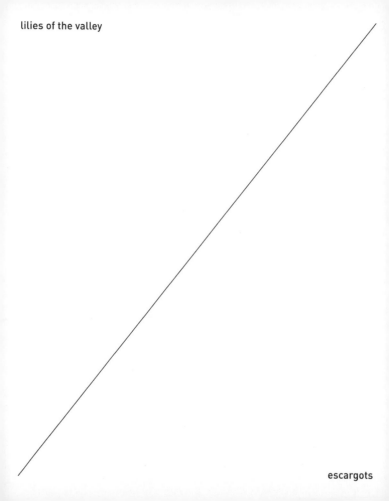

escargots

the view down the middle of the Champs-Élysées

a *Les Mis* poster

Coco Chanel

delighting in a Nutella crêpe

a chic woman in a tuxedo

downing *un express* at the bar

---

flirting on the Metro

elbow-length gloves | impeccably dressed

Julia Child doing her shopping

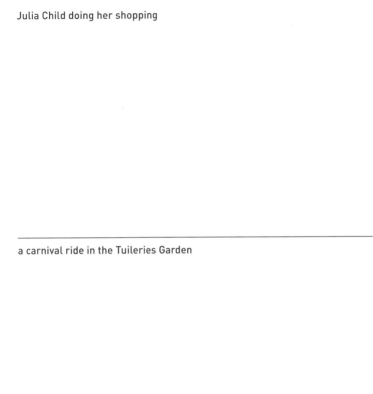

a carnival ride in the Tuileries Garden

Hemingway's seat at Closerie des Lilas

a little girl eating a *pain au chocolat*

false eyelashes	gem-encrusted heels
a MINI Cooper	a *bûche de Noël*

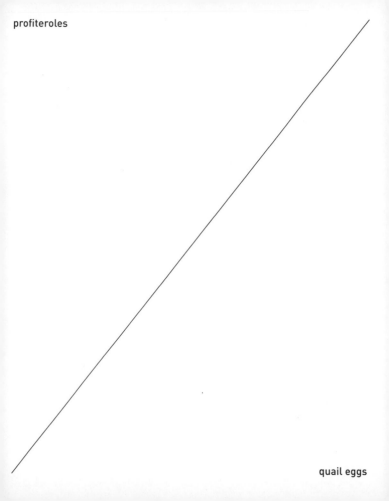

profiteroles

quail eggs

stealing the fancy hotel soaps

"La Vie en Rose"

ice-skating at the Hôtel de Ville

Harry's Bar on a Friday night

Foucault's pendulum

_____

an oyster purveyor on New Year's Eve

effortless chic

Man Ray and Jean Cocteau getting creative

Gigi all grown up

Champagne on ice

a trendy lounge

Marie Antoinette dressed
as a milkmaid

L'Heure Bleue

---

an artfully arranged plate of foie gras

Le Chat Noir

Tintin

Gertrude Stein's artists' salon

kids playing street soccer

Napoleon's tomb

Notre Dame's gargoyles

lovers kissing on the Pont Neuf

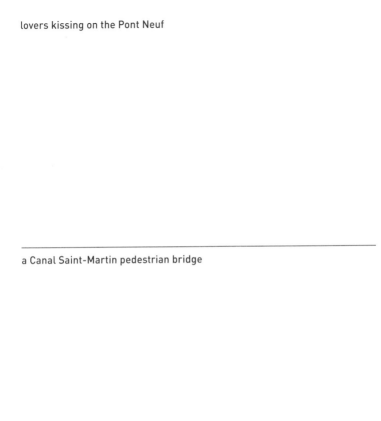

a Canal Saint-Martin pedestrian bridge

| | |
| the *Mona Lisa* | Zola's character Nana |

honeymooners

Louis XIV's bedroom at Versailles

Monet's *Water Lilies*

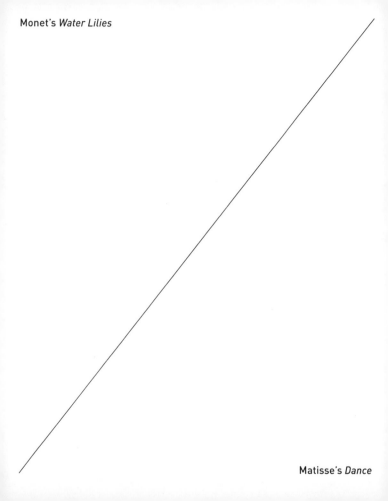

Matisse's *Dance*

Gertrude and Alice

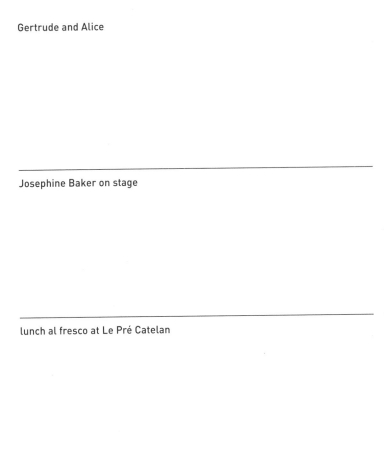

Josephine Baker on stage

lunch al fresco at Le Pré Catelan

old meets new

Napoleon crowning himself

---

oversized designer sunglasses

le Cirque d'Hiver

Notre Dame

olives for sale on market day

passerby nibbling
a baguette

pigs' feet

a bouquet of roses

the Ferris wheel in the Tuileries Garden

old men playing *pétanque*

---

older men smoking

Père Lachaise in autumn

ramekins in three sizes

opulence

Quasimodo

peering out a fogged-up café window

---

looking for love

---

racing to catch the train

Rodin's *The Thinker*

Serge Gainsbourg
looking sultry

shadow and light

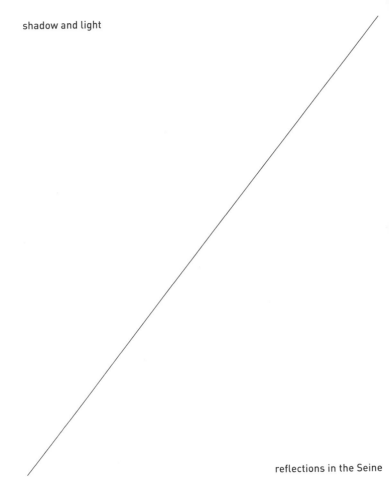

reflections in the Seine

pompiers

a magnum of Champagne

schoolchildren walking
in pairs

a hot dog wrapped
in puff pastry

Sacré-Coeur

ratatouille

---

an accordion

---

sunning in a green metal park chair

Sartre and de Beauvoir's side-by-side graves

---

an old-fashioned candy shop window

Shakespeare in the park

_____

rocking shorts and ankle boots

Paris in the springtime

taxidermy

Robespierre

rush hour at Saint-Lazare

steak tartare

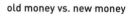

old money vs. new money

| Sabrina post-Paris | the elderly Colette with her cats |

an urban vineyard

_____

room service

sunrise

---

tango lessons on the banks of the Seine

the daily specials menu handwritten on a chalkboard

sole meunière

the Colonne de Juillet

the Batobus

steak-frites

the Brasserie Lipp street sign | the dome of Les Invalides

the bottom of the Pyramid | the chestnut trees in winter

Sunday bike racers in the Bois de Boulogne

teatime in the Paris Mosque courtyard

---

the book stalls lining the Seine

the crowds during *les soldes*

roses and perfume at Costes

the truncated black-and-white columns outside the Grand Palais

strolling hand in hand

the entrance to Maxim's

the flower market in spring

the Eurostar leaving the station

the "empathicalists" in the film *Funny Face*

---

the gate to the Luxembourg Garden

---

dancing in the street at the Fête de la Musique

the hot air balloon in the Parc André Citroën

the French flag flying in the breeze

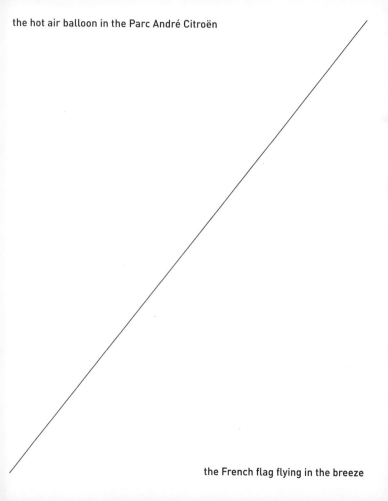

the column of the Place Vendôme | the Eiffel Tower lit up at night

the electro-rock scene at the Plaza Athenée bar

---

the Flame of Liberty Memorial to Lady Diana

---

the elevated Metro crossing the Seine

the Catacombs

_____

the external escalators at the Centre Pompidou

Paris Match

the fountain outside Saint-Sulpice

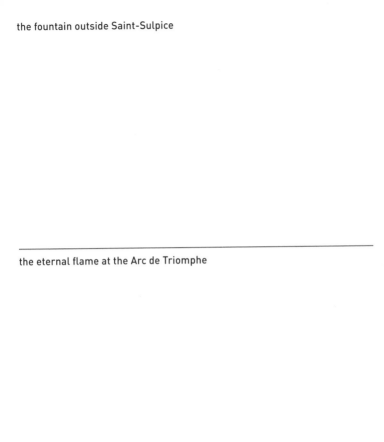

the eternal flame at the Arc de Triomphe

a slice of tarte Tatin

---

the greenhouse at the Jardin des Plantes

the Étoile at rush hour

the arcades of the Palais Royal

a cookware display at E. Dehillerin

the glass dome at the
Galeries Lafayette

a lady in a cashmere wrap

Henry Miller and Anaïs Nin

the Gare du Nord

the Moulin Rouge windmill

the packed shelves of
Shakespeare and Company

the statue of Balzac
in his dressing robe

the Belle Époque interior of Le Train Bleu

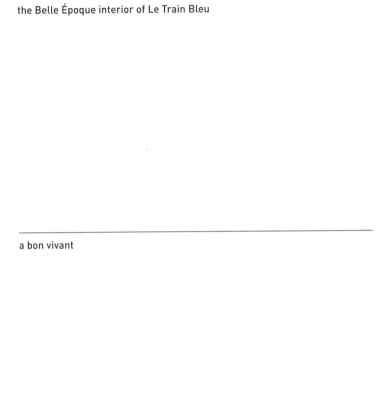

a bon vivant

the Marly Horses

---

the Montmartre funicular

---

a *tabac* sign

the Paris Saint-Germain
soccer team logo

the stained glass of the
Sainte-Chapelle

the Géode at la Villette

the sandbox in the
Place des Vosges

the Seine on a foggy morning

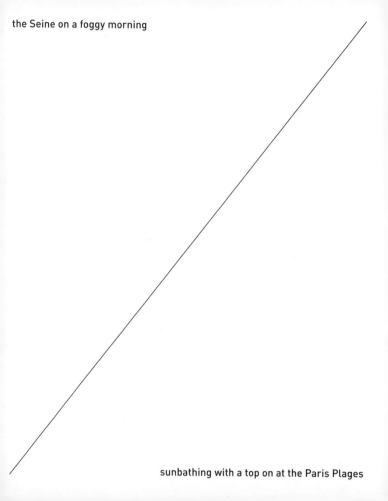

sunbathing with a top on at the Paris Plages

a Paris snow globe

the stamp market

the royal suite

the stage set of *La Bohème*

the Tour de France finish line

the exterior of the Café de Flore

---

the window display of Colette

---

fans watching the World Cup

the Madeleine | the statue of Ben Franklin

the Stravinsky Fountain | the Panthéon

timeless style | the phantom of the opera

the terrace scene at the Palais de Tokyo

the Trocadéro fountains

a bistro table for two

Marianne, symbol of France

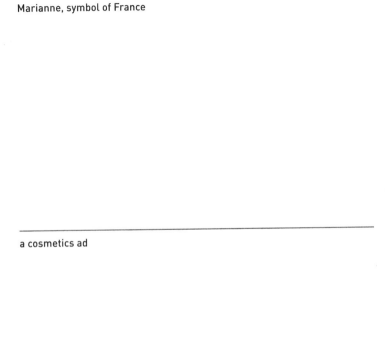

a cosmetics ad

the view from an attic window

---

a ballerina getting off work

toy sailboats in the Luxembourg Garden pond

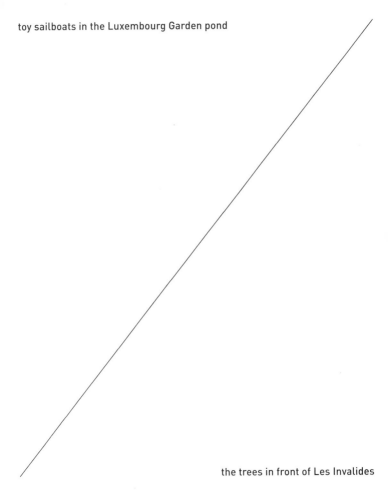

the trees in front of Les Invalides

Versailles's Hall of Mirrors

tourists taking selfies | *Venus de Milo*

white asparagus | a leopard-skin coat

a string quartet

---

the tower of Montparnasse

too-cool local teens

two people riding a bike

wide-eyed tourists

zoning out in the Metro

jet lag

inside the Louvre

---

the vaudeville theater

a *café noisette*

---

the Vuitton Museum

---

a trench coat worn with insouciance

potted geraniums

---

toasting to the next time